7 Day eBook Writing and Publishing System

How to Write and Publish an eBook and Start Getting Sales in Just One Week.

This amazing guide will lead you through every step of the writing and publishing process, all the way to your first sale.

And all in just 7 days!

By Ruth Barringham

Published by Cheriton House Publishing

Australia

Copyright © 2014 Ruth Barringham

Republished 2019

Updated 2023

All rights reserved.

This publication is copyrighted and must not be loaned out, sold, or otherwise distributed by anyone other than the publisher.

This work is copyright. Apart from any use under the Copyright Act 1968, no part may be reproduced by any process, nor may any other exclusive right be exercised without the permission of Ruth Barringham.

This book is sold subject to the condition that it shall not, by way of trade or otherwise, be lent, re-sold, hired out or otherwise circulated without the author's prior consent in any form of binding or cover other than that with which it is published and without a similar condition including this condition being imposed on the subsequent purchaser.

ISBN: Paperback: 978-0-6457543-2-2
       eBook: 978-0-6457543-3-9

Cover image courtesy of khunaspix, FreeDigitalPhotos.net

Also by Ruth Barringham

How to Quit Smoking
How To Write an Article In 15 Minutes Or Less
Goodbye Writer's Block
Living The Laptop Lifestyle
Mission Critical for Life
Self Publish Worldwide
The 12 Month Writing Challenge
How To Have More Money Now
Stop Procrastinating

The Monthly Challenge Writing Series
Book 1 - Quick Cash Freelance Writing
Book 2 - Build A Lucrative Niche Website
Book 3 - Fast & Profitable Article Writing
Book 4 - The One Month Author

See more of my books at
https://www.cheritonhousepublishing.com

Disclaimer:

The Author and Publisher have used their best efforts in preparing this book. The Author and Publisher make no representation or warranties with respect to the accuracy, applicability, fitness, or completeness of the contents of this book.

The information contained in this book is strictly for information purposes. Therefore, if you wish to apply ideas contained in this book, you are taking full responsibility for your actions. Whilst we hope you find the contents of this book interesting and informative; the contents are for general information purposes only and do not constitute advice. We believe the contents to be true and accurate as at the date of writing but can give no assurances or warranty regarding the accuracy, currency, or applicability of any of the contents in relation to specific situations and particular circumstances.

Any links to third party websites are provided solely for the purpose of your convenience. Links made to websites are made at your own risk and the Author and Publisher accept no liability for any linked sites. When you access a website, please understand that it is independent from the Author and Publisher and the Author and Publisher have no control over the content of that website.

Further, a link contained in this book does not mean that the Author or Publisher endorses or accepts any responsibility for the content or the use of such website. The Author and Publisher do not give any representation regarding the quality, safety, suitability, or reliability of any of them or any of the material contained within them. Users must take their own precautions to ensure that what is selected for use is free of such items as viruses, worms, trojan horses and other items of a destructive nature.

All websites, products and services are mentioned, without warranty of any kind, either express or implied, including, but not limited to, the implied warranties of merchant ability and fitness for a particular purpose.

Table Of Contents

Disclaimer: 4
Table Of Contents 5
Why Write an eBook Quickly? 1
First Things First 4
    Doing the Math 5
What You Need Before You Can Begin Writing 7
Where to Begin 13
Your Focusing Statement to Beat Procrastination 15
Your Ebook Blueprint 18
    Writing Your eBook Blueprint 22
How To Write a Sales Page 27
Writing Your eBook In a Matter of Hours 33
    How to Write Quickly 35
    Relax While You Work 37
Second Draft 39
Publishing Your eBook 45
    What To Do Next 47
How to Make Sales Quickly 53
What to Do Next 59
Build an eBook Writing and Publishing Business 62
    Where to Start 62
    What Next? 63
How to write a short report or eBook in just 2 hours. 65
    2 Hour Short Report Writing 67
    How to Research Fast 68
    Writing Your Report 70
    Things to Remember 72

Why Write an eBook Quickly?

Hello and welcome to this brand new book for writers.

What you're about to discover is how to write an eBook fast and start getting sales in just one week.

Think that's impossible?

Well, it's not. I know because I've done it. And not just once. I have the whole system down to a fine (and fast) art.

This book is going to walk you through exactly what you need before you begin and then take you through the whole process of eBook writing, publishing, and selling.

Naturally, the type of eBooks I'm talking about are "How To" eBooks that are usually about 15,000 words in length or less.

But why write them?

If you can write an eBook in a week AND make sales, you're on your way to building a lucrative writing and publishing business, one that you can take with you on the road and work from almost anywhere.

And done correctly, it can be highly profitable too.

Just to show you how profitable it can be, as an example, when Dr Joe Vitale published his eBook "Hypnotic Writing" he sold 100 copies in only one hour. And his eBook wasn't cheap at $29.95 a copy. And in 3 months this one eBook alone earned him an impressive $45,000.

Top copy writer, David Garfinkel, published an eBook called "Killer Copy Tactics" that earned him $35,000 in sales in only 2 months, but both authors were also masters at selling. And while these are two great achievements, you need to understand that these writers weren't new to this business and had been doing at this type of work for years.

But that doesn't mean that you can't have great success with your eBook too.

Just don't think it will be easy though, because it WILL take work, although once you understand, and have worked through my system of eBook writing and selling, you'll see just how easy and effortless it can be.

The only caveat is that you need to write eBooks consistently. It's no good being a "one-hit-wonder" because that won't last. eBooks, or any books for that matter, don't go on selling in huge numbers forever. No matter what type of books you write, sales eventually fall away. Even the most well-known writers know this and that's why they write a lot of books.

But having your own catalogue of hundreds of eBooks selling all over the world, will feel like income on autopilot because you only need to write an eBook once and it can go on selling for years.

Being an eBook author means that you can work from home with no more long commutes to a job that you hate. And if you can write an eBook every week, you'll soon build up an online following of repeat customers who are eager to buy every book you write. This is a great way to earn passive income and gives you the freedom to live anywhere and any way you want to.

As you work your way through this book, keep in mind that the information presented here is meant as a guide and not a strict set of rules to follow. It's best if you start off following all the advice as it's set out. But eventually you'll devise your own way of working. But once you start following the guidelines in this book, you'll have a great base to start from and you'll have your first eBook written AND SELLING in less than a week.

Just remember though, that it WILL take work so you're going to have to put in the necessary hours to get it done.

At first it will seem hard if you've never done it before so be prepared for one full week of non-stop writing and marketing.

You're going to spend 3 days outlining and writing your eBook and 4 days publishing and marketing it. And yes, it will be intense, but not impossible and not difficult.

Just don't schedule anything else into your calendar for this week because you won't have time.

You need to give yourself one whole week (7 full days) of doing nothing except working your way through this book.

If you don't feel up to working hard this week, then stop reading now and go back to whatever you usually waste your time on.

On the other hand, if you're 100% dedicated to earning money as an eBook author, then let's get going.

First Things First

Before you begin, you need to have an idea for an eBook, or even better, an idea for a whole series of eBooks. You work your way through from idea to outline to eBook and repeat the process. And don't forget how important it is to repeat the process. When you finish one eBook, start making plans for the next one to keep the production process going.

But as I said, you need to already have an idea for an eBook or for a series of eBooks.

You also need to be able to write. I'm going to be showing you the process of how to write and publish an eBook quickly, but you must already be able to write. This is not a lesson about how to write, but a lesson in the steps necessary to write, publish and market an eBook in 7 days.

And you must never, ever procrastinate. There is actually no such thing as procrastination. It's just laziness. We all have days when we don't feel like working and it's during these days that some people use the procrastination excuse so that they can sit around and do nothing.

If you're one of these people who always makes excuses to not write, then this system won't work for you. In fact, nothing will work for you because you're too lazy to start anything or to keep going. Sorry if that offends, but it's the truth. Call it tough love if it makes you feel better.

You also need to be able to create a detailed outline for each eBook and to learn to not be too fussy about your writing and understand that good enough is good enough. Don't even try and strive for perfection. It's just another excuse to procrastinate.

You're going to be writing a lot of eBooks and writing them quickly. So, if you get too hung up on worrying that your books won't be perfect, you'll never achieve your goal of writing many eBooks or even one.

It's better to write and publish 10 okay eBooks, than to write and publish zero perfect eBooks.

There's no such thing as perfect. It doesn't exist so don't try and aim for it.

You just need to aim to write short eBooks that people want to read.

People buy "how to" eBooks because they're looking for information about how to do something.

If you write an eBook full of literary prose and deep explanations that they can't understand, they'll not only be disappointed and angry, but they'll probably demand a refund and never buy from you again.

So, remember KISS (Keep It Simple Stupid) and get your information across clearly and succinctly.

Good enough is good enough.

And now that you understand everything, it's time to get to work.

Doing the Math

The first step in your new eBook writing business is understanding that you need to do the work. You need to be creating an eBook every week or two. I say every week or two because very few people can keep up the momentum of writing an eBook a week. I can write an eBook in a week, but I've never done it week after week.

It also helps if you use every alternate week to market your eBook to make sure you get it in front of as many people as you can. Marketing can be more important that the actual writing.

If you can write an eBook every 2 weeks, that's 25 eBooks a year. If you can write an eBook every week, that's 50 eBooks a year, if you take an annual 2-week break. And you'll need it.

You could begin with a "BANG" and write an eBook a week in in the first 6 months) and then slow it down to one eBook every 2 weeks after that, it means that you'll write and publish 75 eBooks in 2 years. And it's easy to see how that's going to increase your writing income considerably.

I hope you can now see the huge potential of writing and publishing eBooks quickly.

Of course, this way of writing and publishing won't be suitable for fiction writing (unless you want to write romance novels which are usually pretty short), but if you did want to be a novelist, it's still possible to write a novel every month which is 24 novels in 2 years. Imagine that!

But right now we're talking about writing short "How To" eBooks.

So let's get started.

What You Need Before You Can Begin Writing

Before you can write the first word of your eBook you need to have these three essential tools in your writing 'toolbox.':

- A great idea
- Motivation
- Focus

The first one you need, a great idea, speaks for itself. If you don't have an idea what to write an eBook about, then you can't write it. And if you want to have a never-ending supply of ideas, you can read my other book for writers, **"Goodbye Writer's Block: How to Be a Creative Genius and Have an Abundance of Ideas."**

But motivation and focus are also extremely important because without them, you won't have the self-discipline to sit down and write.

There is a saying that "discipline weighs ounces while regret weighs tons" and it's true. Sitting down and writing when you don't feel like it, is easy compared to carrying the weight of regret of not doing it.

And discipline begets motivation. In other words, once you sit down and start working, you soon feel motivated to keep going.

Most well-known writers don't write all the time. They only write for a few hours a day. Dan Kennedy only writes for 3 to 4 hours a day. Eugene Schwartz also only worked for 3 and sometimes 4 hours a day. Stephen King for only 2 hours a day.

The secret is how they write. They sit and work with the focus of a Zen monk. They don't get up. They don't let themselves be distracted. They ignore everything and just write. They are also highly organized which means they prioritize their writing time and know what they'll be writing before they even sit down because they plan it out the day before. And even when the words won't come, they stay at their writing desk till they do.

You need to make sure that you have the self-discipline and motivation to sit down and write EVERY DAY too. No excuses. If you don't write you won't make any money. But if you have the discipline to write every day, your income can be almost limitless.

But as well as being able to sit down and write every day, you need to write fast. To do this you need the right environment to work in and the right equipment.

If you like to listen to relaxing music while you work, make sure you have it available. If you like the sound of running water, invest in a water feature. If you need a new computer or a light-weight computer to take with you on the road, invest in that.

Don't ever think of spending money on your writing business as an expense. It's an investment.

If you find it difficult to sit and write for long stretches of time, use the Pomodoro technique for working. This means setting a timer for 25 minutes and when it rings, get up and do something else for 5 minutes and then come back and do it again. Each 25-minute window of working is called a Pomodoro. The late, great copywriter, Eugene Schwartz, used to work in segments of 33 minutes and 33 seconds with 5-minute breaks in between.

These short time spans are meant to make it easier to sit down and get to work because you know you only have to work for a short time. It also helps you to work fast when you're working against the clock because it leaves no time for distraction.

So, if you want to write an eBook fast and start making sales in just one week, you need to be able to turn up and work every day. That's the most important part. Just turn up. Don't make excuses or pretend that something else is more important.

You'll always be ready for work if you make it a habit to just show up every day. Block time out for writing every day. Use Pomodoros if it helps. The good working habits you build up now will carry you through for years. Just don't start off with bad habits. Show up and write every day. Just do it. No excuses.

And now we're going to dive straight into the 7-day writing and publishing system. Each chapter is set out with the things you have to do, which days you will be working, and how long you have to do it all.

So all you have to do is follow along.

Now turn the page and let's start writing.

Days 1 to 3

Where to Begin

Today is going to be a busy day for you so don't waste time doing ANYTHING except what you're supposed to be doing.

Don't check your emails several times a day. Turn your email alerts off. Don't surf the net or read regular blogs. Don't answer the phone and don't turn the TV on.

If a friend calls round for coffee, tell them you're busy, or better still, don't answer the door. If you can, turn off your internet, or at least turn it off on your computer.

I set my phone to Do Not Disturb. I've also set my favourite callers list as an exception (my children and my husband), but they know not to call me during my writing hours unless it's an emergency. This is an ideal set up so that I can concentrate on my writing with no distractions. You need to do something similar to keep your writing mind focused.

I cannot emphasize enough how important it is to do nothing else but write during your writing time.

Just start working today and for the next 7 days. There's a lot to do and you cannot afford to be distracted.

If you've never attempted anything like this before, and never set aside a whole week to work 100% focused on one task, you'll be blown away by how much you can achieve in such a short space of time when you really apply yourself.

But you really need to concentrate and not let your attention be diverted. You can work in short bursts if you want to and take a 5-minute break in between, (Pomodoros), but make sure you sit straight back down again and get back to work.

It will be fun. I promise. And by this time next week, you'll be punching the air with happiness because not only will you have written an eBook, but you'll already be making sales.

This first day though, may seem like there is too much to do. But there isn't, and you'll realize this once you start working.

Today you are going to write your focusing statement, your eBook blueprint, and your sales page.

Think it can't be done in just one day?

Well, it can.

So read on and I'll show you how.

Your Focusing Statement to Beat Procrastination

Time: 30 minutes or much less.

Remember when I said I don't believe in procrastination, and I think it's just an excuse for being lazy?

Well, I still believe that 100%. But I know that there are others who don't so that is why I used the word "procrastination" in the title of this chapter and not "laziness." But pick whichever one works for you.

I am well aware though, that once your mind gets into the mood to not think any more, it can seem impossible to push through it. But you can. All you have to do is take a short break (5 minutes will do it) away from your computer and any other screen, and then sit down and get back to work. DO NOT look at your phone during your break. Make a drink, pat the dog, stare out the window. Do anything but keep standing up and don't look at a digital screen.

Feeling distracted and not in the mood to work, is only a temporary feeling, and it can pass quickly if you let it and deep dive back into your work no matter how reluctant you're feeling.

But one way or another we all need a bit of motivation to help keep us working, especially when the going gets tough.

Understanding why you want to write an eBook is the key to keeping you stay motivated and on track to writing it. Understanding also helps with ANY project you undertake even if it's decorating your house or starting a vegetable garden. If you understand why you want to do it, you'll be more likely to do it. And if you don't know why you want to do something, then it's probably the wrong goal for you.

Once you understand your own reasons for wanting to do something your enthusiasm will show in your work. So if you're writing a book, your enthusiasm to get your ideas across will help your readers to understand what you're trying to teach them.

This is why you need a focusing statement. You need to understand your own reasons for doing what you're doing.

This whole concept may sound a little "hokey" and a waste of time. But believe me, it isn't. If we always just stopped and asked ourselves why we're doing something before we do it, we'd be a lot better off than we are now.

Imagine if you asked yourself why you wanted to eat that huge slab of cheesecake or why you wanted to have a few more drinks or why you wanted to drive drunk or why you're so angry with the kids? Wouldn't you make different (and better) choices if you could answer yourself truthfully as to why you're about to do something?

So don't skip this step because it IS important.

Writing out your focusing statement of why you want to write an eBook (or a whole catalogue of eBooks) will give you a goal to work towards. If you don't have a goal, you won't do the work because you'll have nothing to aim for.

So take a few minutes, sit down, and write out your focusing statement.

- Ask yourself, why you want to write an eBook. Is it money? Financial freedom? Lifestyle? Accomplishment? You can have as many reasons as you want. And for each answer you give yourself, ask why, and then ask why again.
- Do you want to earn money?
- How much money do you want to earn?
- Do you want your book to change lives?
- Do you want to be known as an expert?
- Do you want your eBooks to help you in your business?
- Do you want to be a full-time author?
- Do you want to quit your job?
- Do you want the freedom to work and live anywhere?

- Do you want to sit and write for a living?
- Have you always wanted to be a writer?
- Is it simply because you love to write?

For instance, if you write that you want to earn a passive income from writing eBooks, ask why? You may even find that you don't know why you want to earn a passive income. But think about it anyway. Eventually you might realize that the reason you want to earn a passive income is so that you can work from home. Why? The answer to that could be anything, depending on your circumstances. Just keep writing answers and asking why again and eventually you'll get to the truth. It will be a real "a-ha!" moment.

And that is your focusing statement. That is what you really want to achieve from writing eBooks.

This whole exercise needn't take a long time. You could discover your true reasons in a matter of minutes. On the other hand, you might discover that you have no idea at all why you're doing what you're doing so you may have to sit and think deeply about it.

But like I already said, this is not some sort of guru nonsense where you need to sit cross legged on the floor inhaling incense and chanting.

This is a serious part of the process of being able to write an eBook and start getting sales in just one week.

Because if you don't know why you're doing it, you'll lose the motivation to do it because you just can't see the point if you have no goal to aim towards.

Just take a bit of time right now to sit and write out your own personal focusing statement. And don't worry about what your reasons are. This statement is for your eyes only. So dream big. Dream so big that if you achieved your goal, it would blow your mind.

My focusing statement was this:

I want financial freedom and I love to write.

(To me these go together perfectly)

Your eBook Blueprint

Time: 1 to 2 hours

In this section I'm going to show you a simple and repeatable eBook outline/blueprint that you can use over and over again to create all your eBooks.

But before you do anything, be sure of how many eBooks you're going to be writing. You don't have to know the fine detail of what they'll all contain, but if you plan on writing a series of eBooks it helps to have an idea of how many you're going to write and how often.

Of course, how many eBooks you're going to write depends on what you're going to use them for.

The best idea is to write a whole series of eBooks so that when a reader has finished with one, they'll be eager to buy the next in the series. And don't forget to advertise your eBooks within your eBooks so that at the end of the first one, you can place an advertisement for the next one, and so on.

You could also write shorter eBooks that you give away free for marketing your main eBooks. Everyone loves a free download, and you can use the shorter eBooks to market your websites, to market your other free eBooks, and your main eBooks.

And once you start writing eBooks and you set up your own system and blueprint for writing them, the process will become easier the more times you repeat it. So the more eBooks you write, the easier and faster you can write them.

If you keep writing and publishing eBooks and free eBooks, you'll soon have dozens of them selling and being downloaded all over the world.

Can you see the potential for a great income from doing this? I hope so. eBooks can provide you with a passive income for years.

And all you have to do is sit at home and keep writing them.

But before you write your first eBook, you need a blueprint.

When it comes to creating things, a blueprint is always necessary so that you can focus on your work without having to stop and think about what you're doing and where it's going.

Blueprints are used in many different industries by many different people from builders to dressmakers. They all work from blueprints.

Blueprints can be extremely beneficial when you're writing a book because they save time as well as keep you on track.

A blueprint is a more detailed outline, and a blueprint for writing an eBook is simple and I'm going to show you how I do it.

First of all you need a working title for your eBook. A working title means that it's what you'll call it while you're working, but it may not necessarily be the eventual title of the book.

You just need a title to work with as you're writing. If you come up with a brilliant title later on, go with it. But to begin with your title isn't important. When I was working on this book I simply called it 7 Day eBook, and that was the name of the file I kept the first few drafts in.

Your blueprint needs to contain chapters. Each chapter needs to contain 4 elements. They are:

- Why?
- What?
- How?
- Benefits?

And they're used in that order. You can change them around if you want, but I find that they work best in this exact order.

The reason for using these 4 elements is because your eBook needs to be reader focused. In other words, always remember to answer any questions the reader might have while they're reading.

A better way to explain this, is that readers are skeptics. They won't believe something just because of what you're trying to tell them.

They'll want to know the Why? What? How? and Benefits? of every chapter.

Think of your reader as the cartoon character Bart Simpson, who always asks

"So what?"

"Who cares?"

"What's in it for me?"

And if you use the 4 elements in each chapter, you'll answer their questions.

What the 4 elements actually mean is:

- Why do they need to learn this?
- What do they have to do?
- How should they do it?
- Benefits - How will it help them?

Why? The why question is because it's no good telling someone that they need to do something unless they understand why they need to do it in the first place.

What? Your reader needs to be told what it is they're about to learn. This means the actual concept of your idea for that chapter, plus instructions of what they have to do. This means providing a complete step-by-step explanation of exactly what they need to do.

How? Next they need to know how they are going to do it which means providing a few problem-solving techniques for any problems they might encounter along the way, or questions they might have.

Benefits? Next is the benefits that can be experienced from following your instructions. The benefits section is where you paint a picture of a perfect outcome.

These 4 elements – Why?, What?, How?, Benefits?, - form the skeleton of each chapter of your eBook.

Another reason that they are important is because there are 4 different types of learners.

Why learners, want to know the reason behind needing to know something. To many of them, knowing why they need to do something is more important than knowing how to do it. If they don't have a good enough reason to do something, they won't even try.

What learners, like to know exactly what is going to be discussed and the exact steps of how to do it.

How learners, are more practical and want to get to the nitty-gritty of the exact process of doing something, why certain things must be done in a certain way, and any pitfalls that they'll need to overcome.

Benefit-driven learners, always ask "What's in it for me?" and want to know how things will change their lives for the better.

By covering all 4 elements in each chapter, you'll appeal to every type of learner.

Tony Robbins explained it well when he said that our lives are made up of 2 things; what we know and what we don't know. To understand what we don't know, we need to tie it to what we do know. And this is what is known as our own frame of reference.

So for example, if I told you that you must wear a safety helmet on a construction site, you might not see the point. But if I explained about scaffolding and loose building materials several stories high, you could instantly tie that into your own frame of reference about head pain and brain injuries to then understand the need to protect your head.

And this shows that the difference between remembering and learning, is understanding.

This is what you need to get across to your readers. They need to understand not only what they need to do, but the dangers of not doing it along with the reasons why and the benefits of doing it correctly.

And using my blueprint with the 4 elements of learning included, makes it not only easy to write all your eBooks, but also makes sure your readers understand what you're teaching them.

You see, it's too easy for readers to close a how-to book and say, "That didn't work" without even trying it. But using the 4 learning elements helps to make sure that your readers at least try to follow your instructions so that they can see that what you're telling them does work because they tried it and succeeded by following your advice.

Writing Your eBook Blueprint

So now you need to create your eBook blueprint.

But before you can begin to incorporate the 4 elements of learning into each chapter, you need to know what chapters you'll be including.

So start with 10 chapters, just to keep things simple.

Write a list of 10 topics that you'll be covering in your eBook. Each topic will represent one chapter.

You don't need an exact chapter title, just a list of 10 topics that you'll be covering.

As well as the 10 chapters, you'll also need to add a first chapter, which will be your introduction, and a last chapter which will be your concluding chapter where you wrap up all your information. So you'll have 12 chapters all together, covering 10 main topics.

Once you have your list of 10 chapters, use the 4 elements – Why? What? How? Benefits? - in each chapter.

For each element, list at least 4 answers (topics).

So, for example, if you were writing a book on weight loss and the current chapter was on weight loss through eating more vegetables, your blueprint might look like this:

Why:
- more healthy
- less calories
- more fiber
- everyone has a vegetarian gut

What:
- steam, roast, raw
- vegetables as main part of every meal
- small portions of (or no) meat
- meal ideas

How:
- weight loss through eating vegetables
- vegetable fibre stops you feeling hungry
- stay away from sugar
- less junk food eating

Benefits:
- regular bowel movements
- feel lighter
- never hungry
- weight loss without even trying

You can, of course, add more than 4 answers to each of your elements, depending on what you're writing about and how much knowledge you already have about your subject.

To get a more detailed blueprint, which makes the writing part so much easier and faster, for each of the 4 topics in the 4 elements, write 4 sub-topics you want to include. For instance, in the topic of "more fibre" I could put:

- most diets lack fibre
- all vegetables are naturally high in fibre
- all natural high fiber foods are low calorie and low fat
- sustained energy release

You may also find, if it's a subject you know little about but have researched much, that your research notes contain all the further information you need in more detail.

For instance, in the weight loss example, the why section that contains "everyone has a vegetarian gut" may be something you discovered through research and so you copied and pasted all the relevant parts that you wanted to include in your eBook, into your notes.

So when you come to writing this section, you can simply pull out your research notes and write up your findings from the relevant facts that you gathered.

So, to recap what you need to do:

- Choose 10 topics you want to cover
- Each topic is a separate chapter
- Include the 4 elements in each chapter
- Come up with 4 topics for each element
- Come up with 4 sub topics for each topic

Of course, this blueprint idea is open to variations.

You might find that there are actually 15 topics/chapters that you want to include or only 7. It's up to you to decide what works best for your eBook.

You can also make your blueprint as simple or as detailed as you need. You can also add ideas along the way as you work.

Just remember that the idea here is to simplify the writing process so that you can write your eBook in 3 days. If you make your eBook too long or too complicated, it will take too long to write.

Also, keep in mind that your eBook should address just one problem. Don't be tempted to stray into issues not directly connected to the problem that your eBook is attempting to solve.

For example, if the weight loss eBook is all about different ways to improve your diet, then don't talk about exercise. That can be covered in a second eBook.

The next question is "How long should it take to write a blueprint?"

No more than 2 hours. And that includes research.

There's no reason why constructing a blueprint for your eBook should take more than a couple of hours. It should actually only take you an hour or less if you're completely focused.

If you already know the subject well that you're going to be writing about, then creating a blueprint should be easy.

And even if it's a relatively unknown subject, search engines make it easy and quick to find the information that you need.

If you want some chapter ideas, go to Amazon and use the "search inside" feature to see what other authors are writing about on the same subject and what they have listed as chapters headings in their Table of Contents and use it to get a few ideas of your own.

Just don't get distracted and start idly surfing while researching. Don't click any unrelated links.

Use a timer if it helps and give yourself 25 minutes (one Pomodoro) to do your research. You'll be amazed at how much you can get done in 25 minutes when you're working against the clock.

So far, you should have already written your focusing statement which should have only take you 30 minutes or less, and now you're going to map out a blueprint for your eBook in 2 hours or less.

So it's time to get to work. Remember, set your timer, and use Pomodoros if it makes it easier for you to work.

Just set your timer for 25 minutes and work quickly. When the timer goes off, get up and do something else for 5 minutes and then reset your timer for another 25 minutes.

Working in short bursts like this can be helpful in keeping you concentrate on your work by not over-whelming yourself by sitting and working for too long.

Just remember that you have 2 hours or less to write your eBook blueprint, so you need to get to work right now.

In the next chapter we're going to look at how you can write your sales page and why you should do it BEFORE you write your eBook.

How To Write a Sales Page

Time: 1 to 2 hours.

Once you have your blueprint, it's time to write the sales page, or at least, a draft version of your sales page. You can always go back later and change anything you want.

The reason for writing it first, is so that you know exactly what your eBook needs to contain.

Your sales page is your message to the world about how great your eBook is and how it can help the reader.

And you might get some great ideas while you're writing your sales page about extra things your eBook should include that you hadn't thought about before, which is one of the reasons why you should write it before you write your book. Writing a sales page can be a real brain storming session as you sit and think about how much better your eBook is than any other and why someone would want to buy it.

Your sales page can make or break a sale, so it needs to be good.

Before you write even the first word there are three questions you need to ask yourself:

- Who is your target audience?
- What makes your eBook different to any other on the same subject?
- Why should someone buy it now rather than later?
- So you firstly need to know who you're talking to in your sales letter.

For instance, for the weight loss eBook, the target audience is obviously overweight people. But to make it more specific, the sales page could be directed at overweight people who have tried every other diet and found them lacking whereas this eBook makes it so easy to lose weight without following a special "fad" diet or buying special food. AND it guarantees they won't be hungry.

What makes this eBook different to any other is that the information works with no calorie counting or food weighing required.

And why should they buy it now rather than later? I'd tell them that it's about time that they took back control of their life and that while they're still over-eating they aren't in control. But this eBook will put them back on track to looking and feeling great. But they need to start now and stop making excuses and stop being a victim of the food they put in their mouths. And the first step in taking control of their life, is to download the eBook immediately.

See how I did that? The answers I've already come up became part of the sales page.

Now, the following is how you can construct your sales page.

Start with a heading. The heading can be as long or short as you want. It's best to begin with a question that grabs attention. Perhaps a heading such as:

Are You Sick of Dieting and Never Losing Weight?

Why is that a good heading? Because it speaks to them on their level and it's about what is probably on their minds already. Many compulsive dieters are always of the mindset that "diets don't work" so this headline speaks straight to that belief.

In advertising, they always say that you should start with your prospect and lead them to your product rather than start with your product and lead your prospect to it.

If you start with your prospect, then you can have a conversation with them before you even introduce your product. This is known as the problem/solution approach. You begin by talking about their problem and then offer your product as the solution.

Once you have your heading, you then need to move into a subheading. A subheading further explains your heading and leads them into the body copy of your sales pitch.

So in the weight loss instance, a good subheading would be:

"Does dieting really have to be difficult? What if there was a way to eat normal food, never feel hungry AND lose weight? Wouldn't that be great?"

Again, I'm using questions to get the prospect thinking (and hopefully agreeing) about what I'm asking them.

Next comes the main part of your sales pitch.

The best way to draw prospects in, is with a story. You simply talk about the problem that your eBook is trying to solve, and you "agitate" the problem by talking about how bad it is and how bad it makes them feel.

Then you bring in your eBook and start talking about the features and benefits of it. You can use bullet lists to demonstrate the contents of your eBook and plenty of white space to make it all easy to read.

Lastly you make your pitch and ask for the sale. This is where you explain the urgency and why they need to buy your eBook now instead of later. But don't say "buy it now" or anything else that makes it sound like a purchase. Instead use phrases like "you can download it right now no matter what time it is, even if it's 2 a.m. in the morning." That way it sounds like you're doing them a favour by making things easy and convenient for them.

Your online sales page is your 24-hour sales person. Write it as though you're talking to only one person. Pretend your best friend needs your eBook and you're telling them how great it is and how much they'll benefit from it. What would you tell them?

And don't forget to talk about benefits, not features. Features are what a product is. Benefits are what it does. Benefits are what the customer will gain from your product and how it will change their lives.

A classic example of marketing using benefits was years ago when Apple first brought out their iPod.

Other companies were advertising their MP3 players by bragging about how many megabytes of storage their devices had, which was more about the features of the product rather than the benefit for the customer.

And although Apple's iPod was no better or bigger than the other products, their marketing made it an easy choice to buy because it only addressed the benefit for the customer with "A thousand songs in your pocket" and the iPod instantly out-sold all other MP3 players on the market.

Another good example were some ads on TV for the Chrysler Jeep when it first came out. Those ads were a perfect example of how benefit-driven advertising works. Those ads told you nothing at all about the Jeep, only about the customers who buy them.

There was one ad where a man sees that his neighbour's yard is heavily overgrown and the whole house looks as though the owners haven't been home in months. He asks his wife "What happened to the neighbours next door?" She looks at him as though she can't believe he doesn't know and says, "They bought a Jeep" and suddenly he nods and understands.

There was also another Jeep ad where a boy of about 9 or 10 is sitting in the front yard when his father pulls up in a new car. The boy says, "You bought a Jeep." The father says "Yep. I bought a Jeep." The boy looks over at their small boat with an outboard motor, sitting on a trailer by the side of the house, and says, "We're going to need a bigger boat."

Those ads are genius. All about the benefits of how great the Jeep owners feel and how it changes their lives and nothing at all about the cars. But the ads worked. There were soon Jeeps everywhere. I even bought one myself.

You just need to show in your sales letter, how your product is going to change lives.

If you're unsure about writing a sales letter, take a look online at others in the same niche to get some ideas.

Your sales page needs to persuade and hypnotize your prospects into buying your product so use direct commands such as "download it now" "you need this" "you must have." Commands don't have to be blatant. Subtle is best.

When you write your sales page, also come up with a marketing plan. It's no good having a sales page if no one knows about it. You need to organise your marketing to get visitors to your sales page. So write your sales page and design a 10-point marketing plan of how you're going to attract visitors to your sales page.

Just sit down and stay focused on what you have to do. Write an outline for your sales page. Just a list of what you want to include in it is all you need, and then write it.

Don't use the 4 elements in your sales page. It only works for writing an eBook, not for a sales pitch. But you should include the 'why' element all the way through your sales page. Tell them constantly why they need your eBook.

Writing your sales page and 10-point marketing plan should only take you a couple of hours or less.

If you write your sales letter the way I described, it should be easy to write because the ideas will flow, and your sales letter will almost write itself.

So now it's time to get to work and write your sales page and 10-point marketing plan. You can write your marketing plan first if it helps.

To give you some ideas, part of your marketing plan could include:

- Social media
- Forums
- Blog comments
- Article marketing
- Guest posting
- Offering review copies
- Reduced introductory price
- Testimonials
- Interviews
- Podcasts
- YouTube
- Affiliates

I'm sure you can come up with other ideas too. The internet offers so many ways to market an eBook.

Just don't take too long to get everything done.

By the time you've finished, you'll have so far written your focusing statement, your eBook blueprint, completed a first draft of your sales page, and written your 10-point marketing plan.

And it's still only the first day.

Tomorrow, you're going to start writing your eBook and I'll tell you how to do it quickly and easily.

Time to complete work so far: ½ to 1 day.

Writing Your eBook In a Matter of Hours

Time: 1 ½ days.

So by now you should be already in the groove of working quickly and accomplishing large amounts of work in small amounts of time.

Doesn't it feel great?

And today it's time to get down to the nitty gritty of writing your eBook.

You have 3 days to do it but that includes the work you've already done yesterday PLUS proofing and publishing. This means that you have one and a half days to write your eBook and half a day to proof-read and publish it.

But don't be put off by how much you still have to do because I'm going to show you how easily it can be done.

The biggest barrier, IMHO, that most people come up against before they even start writing an eBook, is that they think it's a huge task and will take weeks to complete.

But if you already have your blueprint written, it makes it so much easier, and faster to write your eBook.

Just remember that we're not talking about writing a huge eBook, but a 15,000 to 20,000 word "How To" eBook (like this one). And it doesn't even need to be THAT long.

Usually, there is an average of 350 words per typed A4 page, if you're writing one paragraph after another, although in eBooks, you often use bullet lists, subheads, and other ways to lay out your work, which makes it much less than 350 words per page. However, pages containing several large paragraphs of text can contain between 400 and 450 words, so 350 is a good average.

This means that every 1,000 words is, on average, 3 pages of writing, so a 15,000-word eBook will be around 50 pages long and a 20,000 word eBook will be 60 pages long.

When you add in the prelim pages (cover, copyright, disclaimer, title, etc.) and the end pages (ads for your other eBooks and associated products) it adds up to several pages more, so your eBook will end up being quite a decent length.

The next question, of course, is how long will it take to write an eBook of this length?

The average typing speed of most writers is 1,500 w.p.h (words per hour). And this isn't fast because it's only 25 wpm (words per minute) which means hitting only one key every 2 to 3 seconds. Even typing at this speed (slowness?) means that you could write a 15,000-word eBook in just 10 hours.

Which means that, because you have one and a half days to write your eBook, you could do it by writing for 6 hours today and 4 hours tomorrow.

Of course, you could do it much faster because, as I said, 1,500 w.p.h. isn't fast. It's only 25 wpm. You could easily double that speed to 50 wpm and write your eBook in 5 hours which means it's even possible to finish it by the time you go to bed tonight, depending on how dedicated you are. Writing it quickly will give you more time for proofing and publishing.

And 50 wpm isn't fast either. Most people can type at around 80 wpm, but you also need to have a bit of thinking time added in, so working at 50 wpm would be ideal and easily "do-able."

I find that working in Pomodoros is helpful for this type of work when I want to sit and write an eBook quickly. It breaks it up well and it keeps my mind fresh when I can walk away from the computer for 5 minutes at a time, and also, knowing that I'm working against the clock helps to keep me focused so that I write as much as I can in the short window of time that I have.

I often start off using Pomodoros but after the first 2 or 3, I ignore the timer and just keep on writing because I'm in the 'flow' and don't need or want to stop. But I still take a 5-minute break every now and again, just to give my mind (and my bladder) a break.

I find it a good idea to have a drink ready before I start so that I can keep hydrated without having to get up. However, once I'm fully into the writing 'flow' I often forget to drink until my mouth gets really dry, but because my drink is already there, it's easy to take a quick drink and carry on working. I learnt years ago not to sit down with a cup of coffee when I write because I hate drinking cold coffee. ☺

But you can work any way you want. Just don't sit and type for too long or you'll suffer from creative burnout. You need to get up at least every couple of hours or so and do something physical - go for a pee or get a drink of water or stretch or walk in the garden or go outside and breathe fresh air or pat your dog.

And because you've already written a detailed outline for each chapter, writing your eBook is easy. In fact, writing is always easy. It's marketing and making sales that's hard.

Just don't start thinking that it's impossible to write a book in 3 days or you'll feel defeated before you even begin.

Many people have written books this quickly.

Famous entrepreneur, Dan Kennedy, once wrote a book in only 3 days.

Dr Joe Vitale wrote his best-selling book "Turbocharge Your Writing" in only one day.

Best-Selling author Stuart Wilde wrote most of his books in only 2 or 3 days.

William Saroyan wrote his Pulitzer Prize-winning play *"The Time of Your Life"* in only 6 days and Sylvester Stallone wrote the script for *"Rocky"* in just 3 days.

And now it's your turn.

How to Write Quickly

Before you begin, make sure you have your outline close to hand and use it.

When you start writing don't stop. If you make a mistake, ignore it. If you think you're going wrong, keep writing. If you don't know how to spell a word, spell it wrong. Everything will be cleaned up in the proof reading.

The only thing you need to do is get your eBook written. Don't let anyone or anything distract you while you're writing.

Immerse yourself completely in your work.

If you feel like it's all getting too much for you, take a 5-minute break and then sit down and get straight back to work again immediately.

When you've finished writing, you'll feel great.

If you're not sure how to get started with your writing, pretend you're writing to a friend and keep the tone relaxed and easy.

Remember the following old maxim if you get stuck. This rule applies to just about any writing you do:

- Say what you're going to say.

Say it.

Say what you've said.

So start with an overview of what it is you want to talk (write) about. Then say it, followed by a summary of what you've said.

Just don't get nervous or you'll stumble and start getting judgmental about your work while you write.

NEVER edit as you write. Writing and editing are two different jobs and can never be done together.

That's why it's important to keep on writing and don't let your mind or your attention get distracted. And don't be too self-critical of your work either.

While I was writing this eBook, I thought that I'd gone way off course at one point, but I kept on writing, all the while worried that I'd have to delete most of what I'd written and start again.

Then I took a lunch break. When I sat back down, I read over my last few pages of writing and to my surprise and delight I hadn't gone wrong at all. I think I just needed a break. What I'd written was fine and quite legible apart from a few typos and grammatical errors. I think it can be writing fatigue that makes us doubt our work sometimes.

This is why writing in Pomodoros can sometimes help, especially on days when you just don't feel like writing but you know you have work to do. Knowing that you only have to write for 25 minutes and then you can stop is easier than thinking you have to sit down and write 15,000 to 20,000 words in one go.

BTW. I keep referring to eBooks as being 15,000 to 20,000 words, but they don't have to be this length at all. They can be shorter or longer. The length is up to you, and it also depends on how much information your eBook needs.

I personally use 15,000 as a guide. Some of my eBooks fall way under this number of words and some go way over. But an eBook should never be too long. People download and read eBooks to get information fast. They don't want to wade through hundreds of pages of useless "filler" information that they don't need.

So stick to your subject and don't go off on a tangent. As an example, many years ago I bought and downloaded an eBook about book publishing. The sales page made it look as though it had all the information I was looking for about publishing printed books.

Sadly, when I read the eBook, a lot of it was about how to write a book. There was nothing about this in the sales page. If I'd thought it was about writing as well as publishing I wouldn't have bought it. But obviously the author of the eBook didn't have enough to say about publishing so they'd filled it with useless information (for me anyway) about writing. Needless to say, I never purchased another of their eBooks. There's a lesson for every writer to be learned here.

Relax While You Work

Something that I always do when I'm writing is listen to relaxation music or to audios with binaural beats that are designed to help with focus and creativity.

Not only does listening to audios help me to focus but it also helps to block out other sounds which keeps me focused on my work, and keeps my mind fully in my private writing world.

And now it's time for you to get to work.

Pull out your eBook blueprint and get started.

Don't forget, when you've finished writing, take a lunch break (assuming it takes you 1 & ½ days to write, so you finish at noon). Walk away from your computer. Go into a different environment (outside, into a cafe, walk the dog) to make sure you get a complete mental and physical break from your work, before you tackle proof reading and editing because you need to read over what you've written with "fresh" eyes.

Believe me, a mental and physical break between writing and proof-reading is vital.

Don't forget that writing is supposed to be fun, so relax and enjoy your writing. You've already done all the 'hard' work, so now you can sit back, relax, and just write.

Start writing now and I'll see you in a day or so.

Time to complete work so far: 2 ½ days.

Second Draft

Time: ½ day.

The first draft of your manuscript should now be finished so it's time to do your second draft. And you have half a day to do it.

This means proof reading and editing your work, and it's where you pick up on errors in spelling, grammar, and typos. Once you've corrected all your mistakes, you need to adjust your formatting to make sure that your eBook is a piece of polished work ready to present to the world.

The concept of a second draft is a mathematical equation that says:

Second draft = first draft minus 10%.

In other words, you shouldn't be looking for things you need to add in, but rather look for things you need to take out.

There's a well-known saying in the writing world when it comes to editing, and it's "murder your darlings." In other words, be brutal in your editing. No matter how well you think you've written something, if there are parts of it that don't belong in your book, no matter how attached you feel to them, delete them. Murder your darlings.

If you've written something that either doesn't help or doesn't fit, lose it.

On the other hand, if there's vital information missing, or a better explanation of what you're trying to say, add it.

Check your sales page too. Make sure it's still in keeping with your eBook and that the writing flows. Now that you have your eBook written, you can add more bullets points to your sales page to demonstrate exactly what your eBook contains. Some authors list their Table of Contents on their sales page.

You can change anything you want on your sales page. For one of my previous eBooks, once I finished it, I changed the heading of the sale page to reflect just one specific example I'd used in the eBook that demonstrated how profitable my advice could be. It was the sales page for my book called How to Write an Article in 15 Minutes or less. And I changed the heading of the sales page to "How I Earned Over $4,000 Writing Articles in Just One Day" after I realised that this would appeal to more readers.

When you proofread and edit your first draft, be ruthless. Use the critical eye of an editor, not the emotional head of the author.

Read your eBook through quickly once and correct any mistakes. Then go through it again slowly to pick up any typos or spelling mistakes you missed the first time.

Don't forget to look out for formatting issues. These can be addressed as you proof and edit or when you finish.

Just remember to NEVER over-edit. You're not trying to turn your eBook into a work of art. It just needs to get its message across clearly and succinctly. It doesn't need to be perfect. Over-editing can ruin your work, and you don't have time to get too picky or over-think anything.

Good enough is good enough. Readers of your eBook are looking for information. If they get it they'll be happy. If they don't get it, but they do get great formatting and no grammatical or spelling issues, they'll be unhappy. So don't undo your great writing by being too critical. Good enough, is good enough.

Also spending too long editing takes up too much vital time that could be spent doing more important things.

If you want to write a lot of eBooks it's important to get your process right. It needs to be a simple process that's easy to repeat. Over-editing should never be a part of that process. Just do what you have to do when it comes to editing and proofreading and move on.

Next, you need to add your prelim pages which are your copyright page, acknowledgements page, and any other page you want to add to the beginning of your eBook.

Also add a Table of Contents. This can be done quickly and easily using Word for Windows or Pages for Mac. It's usually listed in the 'insert' menu. Just place your cursor where you want the TOC to begin and insert it.

If you want detailed information about how to build a TOC there is a free eBook you can download from any Amazon Kindle store called "Building Your Book for Kindle." I wasn't going to supply a link to it because you need to download it from whichever Amazon Store you usually purchase from, but if you want to take a quick look, you can find out more about it at the US Amazon store at http://amzn.to/1CNaqDP for Windows computers and http://amzn.to/1t6lMTw for Mac users. It tells you exactly everything you need to know to format and publish an eBook for Kindle.

Most importantly, you need to create a regular eBook writing habit while creating a simple process of editing, formatting, and publishing. So don't get too bogged down in the peripheral tasks.

Create and maintain a regular eBook writing habit that you can repeat weekly.

So let the "good enough" editing begin and do it swiftly and professionally.

Time to complete work so far: 3 days.

Day 4

Publishing Your eBook

Time: 1 day.

Now that your eBook is written, proofread, edited, and formatted correctly, it's time to publish it.

Where you'll publish it is entirely your choice, but I will say that the fastest place to publish an eBook is Amazon. It only takes a few clicks to upload your manuscript, set your price, etc. and hit "publish." Amazon takes between a few hours and a couple of days to put your eBook live on their site. And while you wait you can start setting up your marketing campaign.

Amazon isn't the only place you can publish your eBook.

You can also use websites like Draft2Digital, Click Bank, and Ingram Sparks. There are other places. You only have to start searching online to find them all.

Amazon is the one website to use if you want to set up your eBook quickly. You can use the "Building Your Book for Kindle" guide to format your eBook correctly before you upload it. You can actually use the information in the guide to format all your eBooks correctly for everywhere you publish them.

Amazon also provides free eBook cover software that you can use online. It's not a bad service but you have to remember that your eBook could end up looking like others that have used the same templates. They also offer a POD print book option for free too.

Another option is to use an eBook cover service provider, but that can get costly, plus you have to wait for your cover to be created.

One option that I use when I'm in a hurry is to make my own eBook cover using Word for Windows or Pages for Mac.

I design the cover as a text document. I find a suitable image of my own or use a free image website like Unsplash or Pixabay.

I then make my cover but I have to make sure it is the right size so that all of it is visible on my computer screen (for reasons I'll explain later).

I position text above and below the image and create a border for my page. Sometimes I use a background colour too. This can all be done using Word and Pages.

I then take a screen shot of the page and save it as a JPEG image so that I can then open it with any image editing software, including the free software that came with my computer. I then make any changes to it that I want and save it again.

Next I copy and paste it onto the front page of my eBook (unless I'm going to publish it on Amazon and then I keep it separate because Amazon places the cover at the beginning of your eBook every time it's downloaded so you don't want readers to see it twice.

A lesson I learned the hard way a few years back, is that if you have a white background on your cover, give it a black border otherwise it blends in on a white page background on the Amazon website (or any website) and looks odd.

If you want to publish with Amazon, their current specifications for eBook covers are as follows:

Requirements for the size of your cover art have an ideal height/width ratio of 1.6, this means:

- • A minimum of 625 pixels on the shortest side and 1000 pixels on the longest side
- • For best quality, your image would be 2820 pixels on the shortest side and 4500 pixels on the longest side

Important: *We cannot accept any image larger than 10,000 pixels on the longest side.*

Keep this in mind when you're creating your eBook cover. It's also a good rule of thumb to use no matter where you want to publish your eBook.

What To Do Next

So now it's time to publish.

I'm assuming that you've already created your eBook cover. If not, do it first. Even if you create it yourself as I've described it, you can have your cover finished in only 30 minutes or less.

You then need to choose your publishing options of exactly where you want to publish it. To do it quickly, Amazon is the "go-to" website.

The big problem with Amazon, is that eBooks don't sell at high prices on their website. So if you want to sell your eBook for more, you can publish it as a PDF or ePub download from your own website. Both Word and Pages allow you to save your eBook file as a PDF. Pages also lets you save it as an ePub file. There are also free online tools for converting Word documents to ePub files. You can also use free software like Calibre to convert any document to any other type of document, including ePub.

You can use PayPal for a payment processor on your site. PayPal send customers to a web page on your site after payment, so you'll need to create a "Thank You" page which includes a link to your eBook. Just make sure that you don't link this page to any others on your site so that the search engines won't find it.

If you don't have your own website (but you really, REALLY should), or you don't want to sell your eBook yourself, you can use an ecommerce site such as e-Junkie or Click Bank who take care of payments for you. E-Junkie also let you up upload your eBook to their website so that customers can download it from there. All you need to provide is a "Thank You" email for which they already have a default email that you can also add a personal message to.

e-Junkie (as well as Click Bank) also have affiliates so you can let others help sell your eBooks and set your own commission rate. e-Junkie also let you upload your sales page to their website too, so you don't even need a website of your own to sell your eBooks. But again it's important to have your own website (or blog).

I used to use Click Bank to sell all my eBooks years ago, but I fell out with them when they kept refunding sales for what seemed like no reason AND without telling me first. There's been a lot of complaints about them doing this over the years from a lot of other people too, so I'm far from being the only disgruntled Click Bank vendor, but you can try them if you want.

I also thought that Click Bank's fees were quite high. At the time the fees were $19 to set up each new product for sale ($50 for the first one and $19 for every subsequent) plus $1 and 7.5% of every sale.

e-Junkie on the other hand, charge $5 a month (at time of writing) for up to 10 products (depending on file sizes) with no upfront fees. So every time you add a new product after the first one, there's no extra charge for the next 9 products. That's what made me eventually change to e-Junkie, their fees are low, and they don't get involved with refunds. Sales are between you and your customer. You can also try them for free for one week.

I once had an experience when a "customer" bought 4 of my eBooks and tried to get 4 refunds and he kept lying all the time and saying that he hadn't received them.

Sadly, one of the sales was through Click Bank so he got that refund behind my back, but the sales through e-Junkie were never refunded. He used 3 different names and 3 different email address to try and scam me, but because e-Junkie let me sort it out myself, he didn't receive a refund on the other eBooks. Even though I attached the eBooks to an email and sent them to him, he claimed he could not access them.

If you're at all undecided about where to publish your eBook, use Amazon to publish it fast. You can always change your mind later and sell your eBook through other eBook sites.

For now though, you just need to publish your eBook quickly so that you know where to send potential readers and so that you can add the "buy now" link to your sales page.

You also need to upload your sales page too. Do that first, even if it's missing the "buy now" links. You can always add "This eBook will be available soon" at the top of your sales page or in the places where you'll be adding the payment links (and you should have several scattered throughout your sales page).

Whatever you decide, just do it fast.

Get your sales page up on the internet where people can find it. Also do a Google search for your sales page so that Google knows it's there and link your sales page to other pages on your website so that search engine spiders will find it when they crawl your site.

Allow a whole day to publish your eBook if you never done it before.

Of course, if you've published eBooks previously, you'll know how to do it quickly and you'll already have accounts set up with the websites that you use.

So now go ahead and publish your eBook.

And next comes the hard part. Marketing to get those sales.

Time to complete work so far: 4 days.

Days 5 to 7

How to Make Sales Quickly

Time: 3 days

This week your only job has been to write and publish an eBook.

But every writer needs to earn money so when you work for a whole week doing just one job (like writing and publishing an eBook), you naturally want to be paid. And the way you make money this week is from eBook sales.

Now naturally, how much money you're going to earn depends on several different factors including the subject of your eBook, who you market it to, and how 'hungry' your market is for the information you're offering, etc.

The best time to start marketing your eBook is before you write it. It's often a good idea to pre-sell your target audience by hinting at a problem they might already be having so that eventually, by the time your eBook is written, they are primed and ready for you to offer them a solution. This works great if you already have a large social media following, or a long email list of subscribers.

And the actual marketing you're going to do now, would have been better if you'd prepared it beforehand ready to send it out as soon as your eBook was published.

Now, if you've published your eBook yourself and you're selling it directly from your own website, then it is already available for download.

On the other hand, if you've published it only through Amazon as a Kindle book, or through another online eBook store like Draft2Digital, then you may have to wait for a couple of days for it to be available..

But all is not lost. You can still start making sales quickly no matter how you published your eBook. You can start your marketing by saying it will be available for download soon and use your marketing skills to wet your readers appetite for your eBook in the meantime. Or use the next day or two to get all your marketing material ready to be sent out once your eBook is available and you can add the link to it where it is online.

You only have 3 days to start making sales (days 5, 6, and 7) so now you need to work fast.

For the time being, we'll assume your eBook is already available for download.

In the chapter on writing a Sales Page, we touched on some of the different methods you can use to market your eBook.

- Social media
- Forums
- Blog comments
- Article marketing
- Guest posting
- Offering review copies
- Reduced introductory price
- Testimonials
- Interviews
- Podcasts
- YouTube
- Affiliates

The fastest way to start making sales is with email, but naturally, this requires you to already have a list that you email to regularly.

The first time I wrote and published an eBook this quickly, I emailed my list straight away with an extremely low-offer price on the eBook for just a couple of days, and it worked. I made hundreds of sales.

You can try this too if you already have a list of subscribers. Just set your eBook up at a reduced price for a week or two (or just a few days) before you increase the price. Then let your subscribers know by sending them daily emails during the introductory low price term.

Another quick way to make sales is to set an introductory low price an send an email to others in your niche and let them offer it to their subscribers. This works if they can sell it as an affiliate. Amazon has affiliates as do some other eBook sites. So let them know that they can earn commission.

Using an introductory low price for your eBook makes it easier to make sales because it adds urgency to your marketing messages, so people know that they have to buy quickly or pay a higher price.

If you email your own list, you can tell them about becoming one of your affiliates too so that they can offer the low subscriber-only code to their email list if they have one.

Another way you can make fast sales using email, is with an auto-responder series of emails. If you work online you should already know how to set these up.

You just write a series of short emails. The series only needs to be about 10 or 20 emails. More is better but around 20 should do it.

In the emails you discuss the problem that your eBook solves without selling too hard. Your emails should also contain some free advice so that subscribers look forward to your emails and don't unsubscribe. And make sure that several of the emails (it doesn't have to be all otherwise it looks like a sales pitch all the time) contain a link to your new eBook.

In my book, "How to Write an Article in 15 Minutes or Less" I told the story of how I wrote 20 short articles/emails in just one day, set them up in an auto-responder series and made over $4,000 in just 3 months. The emails were selling an affiliate product for which I received 50% commission. Imagine how much more money I could have made if I was selling my own product and keeping 100% of the profit.

So if you don't have your own list, you can write a series of auto-responder emails and advertise them for free. Write a short sales pitch for them on a separate web page and link to it from your sale letter.

Blog about your free emails. Tweet about your free emails. Brag about them on social media. Do whatever you have to do to get people to subscribe. Tell them about all the value they'll get and the secrets they'll learn and how they can have it all for free - right now by subscribing!

Also get on a few blogs and leave great comments. Use blogs that allow a link to your website. Most will allow your name to be a website link. Just stay in your own niche or use blogs in a related niche. So for instance, if you've written an eBook on weight loss, you can leave comments on health blogs and exercise blogs or even blogs for new mothers (they often have weight problems for a few weeks/months after giving birth).

You can look up websites and blogs in your own/related niche and offer the owners a free copy in exchange for a review on their site. Look for blogs and websites that do book reviews. Don't pester those who don't.

Or you could offer a free copy in exchange for a testimonial that you can put on your sales page. Just contact them quickly and tell them that there's no obligation and that you're only trying to generate interest in your new eBook and are contacting a few others too. Tell them about your affiliate program if you have one.

Your own blog can be the best place to advertise your new eBook.

You can write short or long articles about the problem that your eBook solves and publish one or more every day.

If you have automatic emails set up to your blog using an email service, people who subscribe to your blog will receive each post automatically by email every time you publish a new post.

You can also use your blog as a place to brag about your new eBook and offer free excerpts to wet your reader's appetites.

They say that you usually have to put your product in front of a potential customer 7 times before they'll buy it. So be prepared for this.

Article marketing works great for eBooks too. Just make sure that the articles you write contain useable/useful information. No one wants to read an article that only tells them things they already know.

If you can't think of an article to write, just use a short passage from your eBook. Pick a few paragraphs of information that can stand alone as an article. Or rewrite a bit of your eBook into a short article.

Some of the article sites that you can use for free are Medium, Hubpages, Ghost, SubStack, or Patreon. There are many others, but these are some of the places where you can start.

Social media can be your best friend when it comes to marketing. If you have a system set up that automatically Tweets or posts your blog posts, it can really help you save time. You can write about your new eBook and your posts are immediately sent to your social media sites. Just make sure you use intriguing headlines so that people are curious enough to click through to see what you're saying.

Or you can go to your social media sites and brag about your eBook and how happy you are with how it's turned out and how much you know it's going to help people.

Once you start looking into the marketing possibilities, you may find even more ways to promote your new eBook.

And I hope that by now, with my suggestions so far and the list of other possible ways to market your eBook, that you have plenty of ideas of how you're going to do it.

But you need to get started straight away.

Marketing is a fickle business. Things can work well sometimes but not at other times. Sometimes something works well consistently, then suddenly it stops working so well.

But one thing you need to understand about marketing, is that it needs to be consistent. You have to keep your marketing machine running on a daily basis for the first few weeks and then you can cut back. But never stop.

You can also use the eBooks that you write in the future to advertise your other eBooks. You can list your previous eBooks in all your newer eBooks with links to them all.

If you've marketed eBooks before then you're ahead of the game. But it still takes time, and you only have 3 days to start making sales. So use these 3 days to get as much marketing material written as you can and then (once you have an online link to your eBook) set it all up to be distributed over the next few hours, days, and weeks. In 3 days you should be able to write plenty of marketing material and visit enough sites for comments, etc., and leave links to your new eBook.

So now it's up to you.

Go through your marketing plan and start working it. Write enough marketing material (articles, blog posts, emails, Tweets, etc) to last a few weeks so that you can start writing your next eBook while your marketing machine keeps on humming in the background.

If you don't have automatic marketing software set up, as long as you have your material ready, all you have to do is publish the next blog post, send the next Tweet, submit the next marketing article, etc., day after day or week after week.

And if you have an email autoresponder set up, it can go on working for you for years.

As Dr Joe Vitale always says, "Money likes Speed."

So...

On your mark.

Get set.

Go.

Time to complete work so far: 7 days

What to Do Next

So now that your 7-day eBook writing and marketing is over, what should you do next?

Do it all over again, only this time it will be easier and faster because you now have all your accounts and systems set up.

You need to repeat the eBook writing and marketing experience because one eBook alone, won't make you rich.

But if you have 20, 50 or even 100 eBooks written in one niche, you'll become known as an expert in your subject.

Let's face it, if you were buying an eBook on a certain topic, who would you buy from, someone who has written an eBook on the subject or someone who has written 20, 50 or 100 eBooks on the subject?

Of course you can, if you choose, write eBooks on as many different subjects as you want. You don't have to stick to just one niche if you don't want to. Many authors write in different genres and niches. The choice is purely yours. Just remember that a series of eBooks on one topic can help to bring in more sales.

The best part of it is that, working at the speed you've been doing so far, means that you can publish 50 eBooks a year (that's one eBook a week for 50 weeks - I let you have 2 weeks off for a break).

And don't think that writing and publishing 50 eBooks in one year is impossible. Many writers have already done it. You can read how my friend and co-author of the copyright infringement eBook, the late Yuwanda Black, wrote and published 50 eBooks in 2011 at http://inkwelleditorial.com/an-eBook-publishing-failure-story-my-quest-to-publish-50-eBooks-on-amazon-this-year.
Hopefully her website is still online and still operational. She also wrote and self-

published 40 romance novels in just 22 months. That woman was a prolific writer and her death in 2021 was a loss to the world.

The important thing for you to do now is to keep writing and publishing eBooks.

Your eBooks don't all have to be long eBooks that you sell. You can, if you want to, write short eBooks that you use to give away for free as "tasters" for your larger eBooks.

These are known as 'viral' eBooks because people like to link to them, or distribute them, to get more visitors to their own websites. You can also contact free eBook sites and send them a copy of your free eBook that they can give away too.

The it works, is that you write a short eBook (which is so simple to do that you can do it in a day) and fill it with links to your other eBooks and your website.

But for this type of marketing to work, your free eBooks need to contain valuable and useful information so that they are a stand-alone product. Many of the big online marketers use this type of marketing all the time.

Your free eBook can also contain links to other free eBooks you've written or to your free auto-responder email series or to your online articles or to whatever will help you sell more eBooks.

I know of one online writer, years ago, who wrote a free eBook to use as marketing to sell her online writing course.

But sadly, for her, the free eBook was full of incomplete chapters which made it really annoying to read. She would begin a chapter, write a few pages, and then say something like "If you want to learn more, sign up for my online writing course."

Can you imagine how many public complaints she received for doing this?

There were people all over online forums whining about how useless the free eBook was and she became famous for all the wrong reasons.

So make sure that when you write a free eBook, it contains really good information so that anyone who reads it will think that if you give away such good information for free, then your paid information must be great.

People may not remember you if you write and publish a good free eBook, but they will definitely remember (and avoid) you if you publish garbage. Even if it was free.

You can also write smaller eBooks to use as free bonuses for your bigger eBooks. But they must enhance your larger eBook.

So, for example, for my previous fictitious weight-loss eBook, I could add a small bonus eBook called "Exercising for Weight Loss in just 30 Minutes a Day" or something along those lines.

Or, if you came up with 12 chapters for your main eBook, you could use only 10 chapters and use the other 2 as bonus products - if they stand alone as additional information.

Or perhaps some information you gathered during your research didn't quite fit in with what you were writing but it could be typed up as a bonus eBook or short report.

But you can make up your own mind, depending on whatever suits your situation best.

You could also add a bonus product to your eBook that could even be an audio version of your eBook that you record yourself. That way, you can sell your eBook for a higher price, with very little extra work.

In the bonus section at the end of this book, I show you how to write a short report (or eBook) in 2 hours or less, which will really help to ramp up your small eBook writing.

Build an eBook Writing and Publishing Business

The great thing about writing and publishing eBooks quickly and consistently is that it soon builds into a regular habit which makes the whole process easier and faster.

Our brains like to establish habits for everything we do so that it becomes automatic, which requires much less thinking. This makes things easier to do and conserves both mental and physical energy.

And you can use this as a basis for starting your own eBook writing and publishing business.

Where to Start

Begin by stating your goal for writing and publishing eBooks. You need to know how many you want to write and in which niche, and where you want to publish them (your own website, Amazon, etc.).

At first, you don't need to know how you'll achieve it, you only have to know that you want to.

For instance, you might have a list of 25 eBooks you want to write in the next 12 months.

So to begin, all you need to know is which 25 eBooks you want to write. Nothing else. You just need to know your end goal.

Once you know exactly what it is you want to do, you then need to sit down and sketch out a plan of how you're going to do it.

Start with a skeleton plan and then fill in the blanks of each and every step you need to take, in what order, and how long it will take to do each one. That way, if you plan for each step of the process and the timing of each, you'll know if you're on track or not, all the way through the process.

If you want to write an eBook a week, which is a hugely challenging undertaking but not an impossible one, you might be better to plan to write and proof-read your first eBook one week ,and format and publish it the next after you've written your second eBook, and keep going like that. That way you won't be rushing to do everything in one week and it will give you time to do other things.

What Next?

You not only need to build a habit of writing and publishing, but you also need to build an online business.

And you can't run a business without systems and processes in place. This is why it's important to have a business plan of what you want to do and how you are going to achieve it as well as how much time it will take to achieve your goals.

To make your goals achievable, you need systems and processes that are easy to do. Don't make them too complicated or you won't want to do them.

For instance, if you have a template for creating an eBook outline, it makes getting started far easier than if you don't have a template and have to start writing an eBook outline from scratch.

What is also important is that once you know what you have to do and the steps you need to take, you MUST start writing straight away and keep going no matter what, if you want to reach your goals.

And when your eBooks are published (and even before), keep your marketing machine going too.

You can learn how to write marketing articles quickly by using my other eBook *"How to Write an Article in 15 Minutes or Less"* which not only tells you how to write articles quickly but also how to write an article 7 different ways (which is a real time-saver) AND 10 different ways you can make money writing articles.

But nothing is going to happen until you start doing the work. You need to set your working hours each week and actually show up on time and do the work.

Don't fall into the trap of trying to make everything perfect before you publish. Remember that good enough is good enough. There's no such thing as perfect so you'll never achieve it.

And if you spend too much time trying to write one perfect eBook, you won't make any money. Being a person with 20 'good enough' eBooks published is better than being a person with one almost perfect eBook.

Having more products means more sales because the industry is product driven. So if you write a few small eBooks and reports you can use them to sell your bigger eBooks or you can bundle your eBooks to make bigger sales.

If you have 50 eBooks, you can advertise your other eBooks in them to help drive sales, because you have a better chance of selling an eBook to someone who has already read one. Repeat customers are always easier to sell to than new customers.

Successful writers have a following of regular readers and that's what you need to aim for as well.

But don't think that once you have a blueprint for everything you need to do that you must stick to it needlessly if it doesn't fit with what you want to do.

Over time things will change or you might find an easier/simpler way to do something or find that something that you're doing isn't necessary or that it's wrong.

Just go with the flow and do more of what works and fix what isn't working and change your method of how you work as often as you need to.

There are no rigid rules, only a starting point.

You may have noticed that I have deviated in this eBook a few times so that I haven't always followed the eBook blueprint that I've been teaching you. But that is what happens. Sometimes things don't fit and have to be changed.

Mix what you've learned so far with what you already know, then use this knowledge to create your own unique strategies and blueprints.

And above all, keep writing and publishing.

I'll see your eBooks online real soon.

Bonus Section

2 Hour Short Report Writing

How to write a short report or eBook in just 2 hours.

2 Hour Short Report Writing

In this short bonus section we're going to be looking at how you can write a short report or eBook (like this one) in just 2 hours.

But why would you want to write a short report?

Well, the most obvious answer is money, especially if you're looking for a fast and ongoing income.

The online industry is product driven. There are many who believe that it's information-driven because most people who go online are looking for information.

And while this is true, it's also true that many people are willing to pay for information, especially if they're looking for a fast answer to a specific problem.

So if you can write a short information-packed report in just 2 hours, it means that working only a few hours a week can produce a lucrative second income.

The problem that many writers face is that they never seem to be able to make much money from their writing.

But if you can write short reports quickly while the others are still complaining, you're getting things done.

And writing a short report quickly, means it can take as little as just one day to start getting traffic and making sales.

And when you've done it several times and produced a few short reports, you'll have a great writing and publishing habit that will make you feel good AND earn you money.

Short reports are great because not only can you sell them, but you can also use them to get more traffic to your website or to build a subscriber list.

You can make money by selling them or giving them away and I'm going to tell you how to do both.

You can also use affiliates to help distribute your short reports which helps with marketing.

Once you start writing short reports you'll see how simple it is to invade any niche in just a few days and start earning money.

But first you need to do your research and find a niche that is profitable.

It needs to be a niche where people are desperate for information.

You're looking for desperate buyers who are looking for a solution to a major problem they're having.

So weight loss, fitness, self-help, saving money, and making money are desperate niches, while scrapbooking and cake decorating are not.

Your niche must also be something that you would be interested in writing about.

It needn't be something that you are permanently interested in, but something that you can at least get temporarily enthusiastic about.

Or as discussed previously, write short reports to give away to help market your bigger eBooks.

How to Research Fast

Once you know what you want to write about, it's time to do your research.

But you need to do it fast. Don't get too picky or linger too long.

There is a need for speed when you research so do it quickly and don't second guess yourself, because once you start to hesitate, you'll start making mistakes.

To find the information you need, look at a few forums and choose the most active ones. This means forums that have many members and plenty of useful answers to most of the threads.

Forums that aren't active means that either there's not much interest in the subject or it's mostly an off-line niche. Either way these people probably aren't looking online for information.

To find the forums you need, type in your subject plus the word "forum" into your browser's search box.

So for instance, if you want to write about dog training, type in "dog training + forum" with and without the quotes.

Choose 3 or 4 active forums and search the threads to find the biggest recurring problem. And by "biggest" I don't mean that it's a huge problem. I mean it's a problem for a lot of people. Something that's being brought up multiple times on each forum.

Next, look for the best answers.

But again, don't take too long.

Altogether, your research should take no longer than 90 minutes.

Break up the time into 3 x 30-minute segments. Every 30 minutes is made up of 25 minutes for research and 5 minutes for a break.

Hopefully, your research won't take this long, but if it does, use the time productively.

Use a timer if it helps.

Once your time is up, stop working, even if you get to the end of your 90 minutes and feel as though you need more information, stop anyway. This will stop you over-researching, second-guessing yourself and making mistakes. With research, your first instinct is usually the right one.

As you research, divide your notes into 4 categories.

The 4 categories are Why? What? How? and Benefits?

This is how you are going to write up your report.

- **Why** the reader needs the information.
- **What** they are going to learn and how are they going to accomplish it.
- **How** what are some of the pitfalls they need to look out for.
- **Benefits** they will get and how it will change their life.

So while you're researching, place your notes under one of the 4 categories.

Take 5 seconds only to decide which information is relevant and another 5 seconds to decide which category it belongs in.

For your How? section, find a few problems/hurdles that people might encounter and explain how to overcome them.

Make as many notes as you need to. It's quickest to copy and paste the information you need into 4 separate documents or write it in your own way.

Writing Your Report

Once your research is done, it's time to write your report. Just remember that you only have 2 hours for this, so you need to make sure you don't get distracted and don't let anyone disturb you.

To write quickly, you need a template. You can't sit down and write fast if you have no idea where to start.

This is where the Why? What? How? and Benefits? categories help.

And because you've already categorized your research notes, all you have to do is write them up into a report.

When you wrote your larger eBook, you put Why? What?, How? and Benefits? into each chapter.

Your short report is going to be written the same way. But because it's only based on one main problem, it's going to be like writing one long chapter but in more detail.

For instance, I previously talked about writing an eBook about dog training with each chapter focusing on a specific problem.

When I researched on the dog training forums, a problem that came up a lot was house training a puppy, or what the people on the forums mostly called potty training.

Potty training was asked about over and over in many different ways and it was easy to pick out the most popular answers. And I knew they were correct because they made perfect, logical sense (and because I've house trained a puppy before).

So potty training a puppy would be a great subject for a short report.

Before you start writing, go through your research notes and put them in the order that you want to write them. So under the "why?" section, if you have 10 notes, number them from 1 through to 10 in the order that you want to write them. Do the same for the other categories too.

You need to begin your short report by explaining what your reader is going to learn and why they need to know it.

So begin by defining your main concept, which in my case would be potty training, in one brief sentence. As an example of how to do it, look at the first sentence of this bonus section:

"In this short bonus section we're going to be looking at how you can write a short report or eBook (like this one) in just 2 hours."

I didn't need to elaborate on this anymore because my subject is straight forward. I then delved immediately into the why? question with:

"But why would you want to write a short report?"

So now go ahead and write up your own why? notes.

Next, write up your "what?" notes to explain exactly what they need to do and in what order.

Next comes your how? section where you should include at least 3 or 4 of the biggest hurdles they might encounter and how to overcome them.

Then lastly, you need to tell them the great benefits they'll achieve if they follow your advice.

Use the benefit section to wrap up the "what?" section and give a few real-world scenarios of changes that can be expected.

End your report with a quick recap of what you've told them to do and then write a "what to do now" section to make sure they use your information and not just read it.

Too often, people download eBooks and read them, but never follow the advice they're given. Then they tell themselves (and others) that your eBook didn't help them at all.

So make sure you conclude your short report with a few paragraphs that explain what they need to do and why it's important to do it right now.

And that's it. Your short report is written.

So to recap on that you need to do and the order that you need to do it:
- Find a profitable niche.
- Find popular forums in your chosen niche.
- Find popular threads.
- Find the main topic for your short report.
- Search the forums for all the threads on that topic.
- Collect notes and file them under the 4 elements.
- Define the main concept of your topic at the beginning.
- Write the why section next.
- Write a step-by-step plan for the reader to follow.
- Include 3 or 4 sticking points and how to overcome them.
- Write up potential outcomes.
- Tell them what to do next.

Things to Remember

While I told you that you need to include why, what, how, and benefits in every short report you write, they don't have to be in that exact order.

You need to exercise common sense when you're writing. So if it suits your purposes more to start with what instead of why, then you need to go with that.

Some writers even prefer to begin with the benefits to really motivate their readers right from the beginning, and end with the why and explanation how bad their life will be if they don't follow the advice.

So do whatever suits you.

Personally, I always prefer to start with the why.

Also remember that you might not be as successful with your first report. You may not make as many sales as you wanted to. Or it may take you a lot more than 2 hours to write it.

But don't worry about it because in the beginning it's more important for you to become familiar with the process of 2-hour report writing because you need to acquire a good technique of researching and writing.

As you keep writing and publishing short reports and eBooks, the process will become easier and faster to do, and your income will increase.

You just need to give it time to work.

But the benefits will be worth it because, when you think about it, this process can't fail.

If you wrote and published just one short report a week, that would mean you'd have 52 reports selling and being distributed all over the world by this time next year.

And if you also wrote 3 marketing articles for each one and included at least 3 affiliate links in each report, that would mean you'd have 52 reports, 156 marketing articles and 156 affiliate links circulating all over the internet in just one year.

And you could accomplish all this by working just one day a week - or less.

That would leave you with plenty of time for other writing (or for leisure).

You could use affiliates to help sell your reports too. Affiliates are great because most of them have their own list of subscribers. So if you had 100 affiliates who had only 1,000 subscribers each they would collectively market your short reports to 100,000 people.

Or you could use social media and email to help market your work.

You could give your short reports away for free to get more subscribers to your website.

You could put links to your main eBook in your short reports and give them away as free marketing.

You could allow others to give away your free reports too.

Or how about using your 2-hour report as a free bonus product for one of your bigger eBooks?

Or you could offer your report writing services to others. Even if you only charge $100 to write a report, you could earn $500 a week in extra income which would be an extra $25,000 a year from working part-time - one day a week, if you only wrote one report a day.

But you could write 3 or 4 reports a day which could triple or quadruple your income up to $100,000 a year.

Writing short reports is profitable if you do it consistently because it means you have more products to offer and the more you do it, the easier and faster creating them becomes.

This bonus section you're reading now was created using the method outlined here.

I may have deviated slightly, but basically I kept to the script.

I also didn't need to research because I already knew my subject intimately.

Writing short reports has worked for me over the last few years because they are quick to create and can go on working and earning money for years.

So now it's your turn.

Reading this short bonus section won't help you unless you follow the advice and actually do the work.

But it's not really work when it only takes 2 hours and writing is something you love to do.

So don't waste any more time wondering "what if?".

Instead, start now and have your first short report written and published before you go to bed tonight.

www.ingramcontent.com/pod-product-compliance
Lightning Source LLC
Chambersburg PA
CBHW050321010526

44107CB00055B/2338